FLASHES *of* THOUGHT

GW01186285

Also by Mohammed bin Rashid Al Maktoum

My Vision
Spirit of the Union
Flashes of Thought
Flashes of Verse

FLASHES *of* THOUGHT

Lessons in Life and Leadership
from the Man behind Dubai

POCKET EDITION

Mohammed bin Rashid Al Maktoum

PROFILE BOOKS

First published in Great Britain in 2015 by
Profile Books Ltd
3 Holford Yard
Bevin Way
London WC1X 9HD
www.profilebooks.com

A CIP catalogue record for this book is available from the
British Library.

ISBN 978 1 78125 503 2
eISBN 978 1 78283 185 3

Text design and typesetting by sue@lambledesign.demon.co.uk

Printed and bound in Italy by L.E.G.O. SpA-Lavis (TN)

Contents

Sheikh Mohammed
and Dubai

Dubai is one of the seven emirates that make up the United Arab Emirates. It began the 20th century as a humble port town home to traders, seafarers, fishermen and pearl divers. It was not until the 1950s, when Sheikh Rashid bin Saeed Al Maktoum became ruler, that Dubai began its journey to becoming a global metropolis.

Born and raised in Dubai, Sheikh Mohammed bin Rashid Al Maktoum travelled to England for military training at the Mons Officer Cadet School. He served as Commander-in-Chief of the Dubai Police Force and later UAE Minister of Defence, was appointed Crown Prince of Dubai in 1995, and in 2005 became Ruler of Dubai as well as Vice-President and Prime Minister of the UAE.

Sheikh Mohammed is the driving force behind the transformation of Dubai into one of the great cities of the modern world: a hub for business and tourism, and the world's gateway to the Middle East. He is also a key figure in establishing the UAE as a success story of peaceful human development and a model of tolerance and moderation for a troubled region.

Sheikh Mohammed's drive for "number one" has produced countless firsts for Dubai and the UAE: Emirates, the world's fastest-growing airline; Dubai World Central, the world's largest airport; and Burj Khalifa, the world's tallest tower, to name a few.

His work behind the scenes is less visible but no less important. Sheikh Mohammed is a proponent and pioneer of open, businesslike, service-led governance: his reforms have earned the UAE the number-one global ranking for government efficiency.

In his private life, Sheikh Mohammed is a world champion endurance rider with a passion for horse racing. He founded the Godolphin stable and the world's richest race, the Dubai World Cup. He is also an acclaimed poet in Arabic, with several published collections.

Driven, ambitious, determined and competitive, Sheikh Mohammed is a national leader, a soldier, a poet and a horseman. This unusual mixture of attributes has created a remarkable man. His sense of urgency and will to win are legendary. His reflections in this book on how to build teams, succeed in business and get the most from life come from a man who has excelled in doing exactly that.

FLASHES *of* THOUGHT

1

Simplicity

The key to happiness is to lead a simple life.
Refuse to be burdened with needless
complexity.

It might come as a surprise to some people, but I try to lead a simple life.

On my days off, I start as always with dawn prayers, a habit I highly recommend. Waking at dawn is not hard once you get used to it; it is as if an inner alarm clock rouses you every morning. After prayers, I have breakfast with my family and then I practise some of my favourite hobbies. I ride my bike or go horse riding in the desert. Watching the deer and the rabbits in the wild gives me peace of mind.

I call on friends at their homes, and we go out for lunch in nearby restaurants or for a walk on the beach. Sometimes we go to visit people or go on hunting trips together. My day is simple, as is my life, but I am happy with it.

Life was created simple and it is important to live it as such. Simplicity is inherent; it leads to peace of mind and tranquillity. I absolutely do not like to overcomplicate things, as those who are close to me know well.

We Emiratis are very fond of the sea and of the desert, despite the intense development and modernisation that can be seen in our towns and cities.

The splendour of life is felt in the warm sun shining over the dunes, in the moonlit sky, in the pouring rain, in the green grass growing on the plains and in the valleys, and in joyful gatherings with friends and loved ones. I greatly enjoy the beauty of running horses.

It is such a beautiful life, but many people spend it worrying, burdened and frowning. You can easily see the beauty of life in the laughter of a child, the tenderness of a mother, the smile of a friend or the love of a compassionate wife.

Our country's founding father, Sheikh Zayed, God bless his soul, was the most down-to-earth of all the world leaders I have had the chance to know. He was also the most smiling and cheerful of all. He loved the beauty of life and sought it in poetry and in prose, on land and at sea, despite his busy schedule and his heavy responsibilities.

My advice to all is to lead a simple life. Simplicity starts in the heart, away from negativity and pessimism.

2

The race to be number one

Intend to be a winner, or you will never win.
"First" is the only goal worth setting.

When I am asked about my continued insistence on being number one, despite the difficulty in achieving this objective in all fields, I answer that nobody remembers runners-up. Who remembers the second person to climb Mount Everest? The second person to walk on the moon? In fact, who remembers anyone who comes in second? The answer is: nobody.

We are no less than number one. Whoever convinces himself that he is not worthy of first position has doomed himself to failure from the very beginning. My people and I are fond of being number one.

This is not a new characteristic, but one that we have inherited from our founding fathers. Sheikh Zayed and Sheikh Rashid both loved to be the first and wanted their people to be the first, too. From the outset they wished to see the UAE at the very top and their successor, our President, God bless him, is following in their steps.

I am not the only one who wishes to be number one. Abu Dhabi, for instance, aspired to global leadership in alternative energy. It invested, innovated, was chosen to host the International Renewable Energy Agency (IRENA), and created Masdar, a city focused on sustainability. As a result, Abu Dhabi has become a magnet for companies and research centres, and a beacon of innovation in renewable energy.

Abu Dhabi also wished to become a cultural capital of the world. Therefore it built museums, hosted cultural events and embraced the finest works of art in the world. Such is the modus operandi of those who wish to be no less than number one.

We have no alternative to first position. The word "impossible" is nowhere to be found in the vocabulary of the UAE.

Today the UAE is number one in the Middle East in terms of infrastructure, human development, technological development, knowledge economy, citizen happiness and satisfaction, renewable energy, safety, security, trade, tourism, and many other areas. We shall continue our pursuit of global excellence in all fields, for we are a nation that accepts nothing less than first place.

Let me explain why it is so important always to aim for number one. If you want to run one kilometre, you will surely feel tired once you finish. However, if you make up your mind to run 10 kilometres, then you will not feel tired after the first, second or even the third kilometre. Your determination and energy will be proportionate to your goal. Therefore, set a high goal for yourself and do not settle for anything less than the very best. The best is exactly what you will get if you accept no less.

Never ever doubt your ability and never underestimate your capacities. Do not take your mind off your goal. Always work towards first position and trust in God, for it is God who grants success.

3

Keys to leadership

*Welcome competition with open arms,
harness ambition to beat your goals
and nurture creativity to generate
new ideas.*

A short while ago I met with a group of around 500 international executives from the biggest companies in the world who came to Dubai for a conference. They asked for a speech, so I told them I would recount three stories that summarise the three most important characteristics to be found in business leaders.

The first story dates back to 1985 in Dubai. An airline controlling around 70 per cent of the air traffic in Dubai Airport asked us to put an end to our open skies policy, which entitled any airline to operate in Dubai Airport. They wanted to protect their market share and even set us a deadline of a few weeks to comply. If not, they threatened to withdraw from the airport, which would lose almost 70 per cent of its traffic.

We refused their request for a simple reason: we believe that competition, and not protectionism, is healthiest for our country. So we rented two aeroplanes and created an airline that we called Emirates. In short, they forced us to establish our own airline, which now ranks third worldwide.

The first lesson to be learnt is that competition always makes you stronger and better. Competition is feared only by the weak. Our country is better because it is open to competition; our employees are better because they compete with everyone; our streets are better because we want them to surpass those of other countries. Even our government institutions become better when we give out distinction awards that encourage competition for first place.

The second story took place in the early 1970s. A group of traders paid me a visit and asked me to dissuade my father from undertaking a project that he had set his mind upon. The project was none other than the Jebel Ali Port.

The traders believed that this project was unnecessary and would only burden the Treasury with huge costs. I spoke briefly with my father, God bless his soul. After a moment of silence, he told me that he was building something for the future, something that we would not be able to build with our dwindling future resources of oil. Today, Jebel Ali Port remains the largest man-made harbour in the world and also ranks among the top 10 busiest cargo ports worldwide. It has more than 60 giant berths and a free trade zone hosting thousands of companies. Moreover, our experience in this field has qualified us to run over 60 ports around the world.

The moral of this story is that we should arm ourselves with a long-term vision, high ambitions and far-sightedness. Without a vision to guide our path, and without ambition that knows no limits, we can never build a bright future for generations to come.

The third story dates back to 1999 when we considered building a business zone dedicated to technology companies. We called the project Dubai Internet City. The investment was modest, but the idea grew to include several specialised zones in media and education, and more. Today these zones encompass 4,500 companies and 54,000 employees, making Dubai the region's capital of creativity in these domains.

This shows us that creativity and ideas can build countries and institutions. The future belongs to those who generate ideas. Today, the UAE is the only country in the region to have achieved official categorisation as a knowledge-based and innovation-based economy.

Our objective is to rank among the top countries in the world. With the help of a long-term vision, high competitiveness, creativity and innovation, we are sure to get there.

4

Positive energy and positive thinking

Positive energy is born of optimism.
Positivity is a choice that empowers us
to set and reach our highest goals.

During my meetings I always talk about positive energy, its influence on our lives and its effect on how much we can achieve. I also mentioned it in my previous book *My Vision*.

I am a believer that all of our actions and accomplishments are simply a reflection of what we bear in our hearts. I believe that positive energy and optimism help us to take up any challenge in life and to succeed in even the most difficult tasks. I also believe that positive energy is contagious: we can transmit it to others. In the same way, we can ourselves be influenced by other people's positivity or negativity.

In the course of my long career, I have seen many

colleagues and friends with negative energy that I just could not change. Whenever I would propose any project, they would dwell on its impossibility or difficulty; and whenever I would come up with an initiative, they would just say, "It is not doable."

Even if I said that the sun was shining, they would answer that they could not see it; and if I suggested that they come out to see it, they would reply that they just could not do so. Indeed, I have met quite a few negative and pessimistic people. I have replaced them in my life by seeking out much more optimistic, enthusiastic and positive people.

> 66 *A positive person is confident that no challenge will stand in the way of achieving his or her goal* 99

I have faced many challenges in my professional life, but never have I allowed myself to be defeated. Does running water stop when it reaches a rock? Of course not. It turns either left or right, and continues on its way. Likewise, a positive person is confident that no challenge will stand in the way of achieving his or her goal.

Start your day with positivity and optimism, with a positive idea and with confidence in your abilities. It will be reflected on your face, in your smile, in your interactions with people around you, and in the way you deal with daily challenges. Haven't you noticed that positive people have a wider smile, a brighter face and a more beautiful spirit? On the other hand, negative people spend their time hiding from challenges and expecting the worst from life.

Positive energy is born of optimism. Our religion assures us that if you are optimistic, you shall find what you seek. If you see the world around you as filled with misfortune, troubles, worries and sadness, so it will be. On the other hand, if you see the world as abounding in opportunity, adventure, happiness, comfort and achievement, it will be that way. It is your mind and your way of thinking that create your reality. You choose whether you want to live your life with positive or negative energy.

Positive energy turns hard times into beautiful moments, hardships into manageable challenges, and the impossible into nothing more than a word or a point of view. It offers you a beautiful perspective on life and arms you with the ambition, drive and motivation you need to succeed.

My advice to all is to arm yourselves with positive energy and to use this energy to raise your team's morale, for a team is influenced most strongly by its leader. Do not undermine your team's morale with pessimism or hesitation. An army's success depends on more than weapons and supplies; high morale can be the key to victory, just as low morale can spell defeat. If morale is high, people will interact with their leader's vision, achieve his or her objectives and follow in his or her tracks. If low morale causes underachievement, the blame will undoubtedly fall on the leader and on no one else. So offer your team optimism and positivity, and they will reciprocate with achievement and creativity.

5

The victory sign

Be creative in everything you do:
even celebrating success!

People often ask me the secret behind the unusual hand gesture that I am known to make at moments of personal victory, such as in endurance horse-riding races. Instead of the customary two-fingered 'V' for victory, I raise my thumb, index finger and middle finger together in a three-fingered salute of my own design.

The universal 'V' for victory is traditional elsewhere around the globe, but not for us here in the Arab world. I thought to myself – why should we always express our happiness in the language of others? We Arabs have a deep-rooted civilisation, a rich language and immense creativity.

Therefore, I came up with my own victory sign. I raise three fingers to express three things: 'success' and 'victory' (which are three-letter words in Arabic) and the three-word sentence 'I love you'.

My victory sign is a simple yet symbolic gesture. It indicates that we should have our own distinct personality, and that we should take pride in our language and our heritage. Creativity should be integral to everything that we do. Creativity should also be intrinsic to our personality, if excellence is what we seek.

I remember more than 12 years ago a work team from a public real-estate company came up with the fresh and innovative idea to build an island in the heart of the sea. Demand for seafront property was high owing to its scarcity, so I approved the idea. After some time, they showed me the plans and drawings of the island, which was in the form of a circle. I asked them why they had chosen this shape. They replied that it was the most appropriate and habitual form, and was recommended by experts. I explained that since this would be such a huge project – the biggest man-made island in the world – we should find a way to leave our mark on it. It should not take a common shape. I suggested building it instead in the form of a palm tree. This would symbolise our heritage and also bear witness to an important dimension of our life on this land.

Today, the Palm Islands are world-renowned landmarks that represent something important about us. Their huge scale, which makes them visible from space, is a symbol of our ambition, our positivity and our capacity to deliver. Their unique and distinguished shape signifies our spirit of creativity, innovation and heritage.

So, I say to my colleagues: if you accustom yourselves to creativity in small things, creativity on a larger scale will follow. Creativity is inherent in a person's make-up and way of thinking. To be creative is to add something new to life as opposed to being a passive part of it. We may not live for hundreds of years, but the products of our creativity can leave a legacy long after we are gone.

6

Bigness

Don't let fear make you small. Think big,
aim big, and you'll achieve big.

In the late 1960s, when my father, Sheikh Rashid, was proposing to build Dubai's first deep-water port, Port Rashid, he decided to construct a maritime zone based around four berths. At the time, some people were very sceptical. They did not understand how a small town of some 60,000 people could possibly need such a large port.

Halfway through the construction, he changed his plans and added 11 more berths. The increased cost would be a challenge, but he was determined to expand the new port. As each new berth was built, it was immediately put into service so that it could contribute revenue to the ongoing cost of the construction. Four years later, in 1972, Port Rashid was officially inaugurated. I was with my father that proud day: not only was the port fully operational, but its 15 berths were all in use, with ships waiting offshore to come in.

Time after time he would describe a new project for the city. And doubtful people would shake their heads. But he would be proved right as our city grew because his vision was big enough to bring that growth.

Later, it fell to me to lead in his place. And because he had taught me never to fear scale or vision, we have created a big city in place of that small town: a city of over two million inhabitants, home to one of the world's busiest airports, the largest man-made harbour and the world's tallest tower. There are many more firsts in Dubai today and we plan many more for the future. Our aim is to be first in all we do.

The point is this: just because Dubai was small, it didn't mean we had to think small. It meant we had to think big. Everybody starts small. We all begin life as a single cell. Every business starts as one person with an idea. How fast you go, how far you get, is in your hands. The bigger your vision, the bigger your achievement will be.

Will you stumble on the way? Perhaps, but we cannot let fear keep us small. We have to be brave to be big.

7
Motivating teams

It is important to empower and reward people, but the top priority must be to listen. Only a manager who listens will succeed.

The first key to motivating a person towards better performance is to empower him or her to achieve. Nothing motivates an employee more than seeing the results of his own achievements. Granting power in this way is also an expression of trust and respect. I sometimes receive complaints in my personal email from employees who spend long years in their jobs without any real power, and therefore without any real achievements that they can call their own. Do not be afraid to give real power to your employees, because you too once stood in their shoes, and if you had not been given the power to achieve, you would not have arrived where you are today.

We must believe in the capabilities of our teams. Every person has tremendous capacities. A true leader is one who creates a favourable environment to bring out the energy and ability of his team. A great leader creates more great leaders, and does not reduce the institution to a single person. We sometimes look for second-line and third-line leaders in an institution, but find none, because the person in charge has not sufficiently empowered his team to bring out and refine their capacity for leadership.

The second key to motivation is the need to reward distinguished and creative employees. They should be held up as examples for the whole institution. Human competition is central to every aspect of our life. Even our religion requires us to compete in doing good deeds. You can never create a competitive environment unless you reward and praise creativity. Praising employees means giving credit for success to them, and not only to yourself. It means honouring their accomplishments and showing your belief that the success of the institution embodies the success of every single one of them. If employees see their leader attributing success to them rather than to himself, they will hold him in high esteem. They will regard him as their role model, not only as their leader.

The third driver of motivation is related to the idea that the job of the government is to ensure the happiness of society. Well, employees are part of this society, and so it is necessary to ensure their happiness in order that they in turn can bring happiness to others.

A happy employee is more productive, more energetic and more creative – hence the importance of creating a happy environment within every institution. In order to make employees happy, we must show that we care about them, we must share in their joys and pains, we must help them to create balance in their lives, and we must add value and motivation to their jobs. Most importantly, we must listen attentively to what they have to say. A successful leader listens to his or her employees, for listening is an expression of respect and appreciation.

It is important for managers to work in this way to nurture their employees' happiness; for one's job is a major part of one's life, and life is too precious to spend in misery.

8

The impossible

There is no such thing as impossible. Everything is achievable with ambition and drive.

'Impossible' is a word coined by those who do not want to work, or rather, those who do not want us to work.

'Impossible' is nowhere to be found in the dictionary of the UAE. It is a word used by some people who fear to dream big. It is like chains that tie a person down, hindering his every move. It can confine a person like a great prison, preventing him from moving around, living life and achieving great heights.

We were told that developing a tourism industry in our hot desert was impossible; today we receive over 10 million visitors yearly. We were told that building towers in the sea was impossible; today we have the biggest man-made island in the world with hundreds of towers housing thousands of people. We were told that our region was teeming with tension and therefore our trade could not thrive; today we are the biggest partner in the Middle East for the most important economies in the world. We were told that bringing Arabs together was impossible; today the UAE has proved itself to be a union of unprecedented success.

> 66 *I have no clue who invented the word "impossible", but it was clearly someone looking for an easy life* 99

The seemingly impossible is not a gauge of our strength and potential, but rather of our faith in ourselves, of our confidence in our capabilities and of our belief. Do not ever allow the word "impossible" into your life, because it would mean that you are weak, or that those around you are weak. That said, the truth is that there is no such thing as a person who is strong or weak – only a person who is willing or resistant.

I have no clue who invented the word "impossible", but it was clearly someone looking for an easy life, a life of sleep and inactivity. We have never had faith in this word. Today I hear the expression "beyond the realms of possibility". It is said that there are three impossibilities in life: first, the griffin, a mythical bird that never lands but is always flying, to the point of laying its eggs in the sky, where they hatch into fledglings in flight and never reach the earth; second, the ogre, of which we have never seen any trace, for it too is a myth; and third, a loyal friend. Mind you, these are not my words, and many people have added other impossibilities to this list, each according to his convictions.

Last but not least, I would like to tell you that the impossible cannot be where there is perseverance and faith. There is no impossible in life.

9

Horse riding, poetry and leadership

Every leader must have a passion in life. Passions define a leader's unique qualities. Passions distinguish a leader from the crowd.

Do my passions for horse riding and poetry contribute to my role as a leader? Most surely.

Horse riding is synonymous with pride, chivalry, dignity and nobility – all of which are indispensable characteristics for a leader. I have learnt a lot from horse riding and horses. I love my horses and they love me too. Horse riding is a beautiful world and whoever discovers it falls in love with it and cannot stay away.

Our love for horses and horse riding is second nature, and this comes from our Arab roots. I would like to add that horse races, particularly 160-kilometre endurance races, require planning, patience and high control – all qualities that should be found in any leader.

Poetry is another world. A poet's eye is bonded to his heart. The eye and heart of a poet are different from those of others. A poet sees what others fail to see. He scans the sky, the sea and the desert unhurriedly. His look is filled with passion and he takes in the beauty of life around him. His heart is very sensitive. He knows his society well, he is touched by its joys and concerns, which he translates into verses full of sincere emotions and poetic feelings. Look at the history of Arabs – we have recorded and passed on our stories in the form of poetry, and we have found that stories told in verse are deemed more sincere and more trustworthy than mere prose.

> **Every leader should have a passion in life that adds depth, uniqueness and style to his leadership**

What I mean is that a poet's knowledge of his society brings him closer to others as a leader. A poet's perception of the aesthetics of life around him is also reflected in his decisions and choices as a leader. Even his projects become lively paintings that speak to people and interact with them, instead of mere rigid projects isolated from the people around them.

Horse riding, poetry and leadership form a triad,

positively interacting with one another to make you a better horseman, a better poet and a better leader. Of course, I am not saying that every leader has to be a poet or a horseman; but every leader should have a passion in life that adds depth, uniqueness and style to his leadership.

10

The Arab Spring

*Change or you will be changed: leaders
who neglect the good of their people will
be forsaken. Leadership is a service, not
a gateway to privilege.*

Nowadays, the Arab Spring and its repercussions
on the region are hot topics at every meeting and
summit. However, these issues did not appear overnight.
The general feeling of discontent and dissatisfaction that
unleashed this wave of transformation had been felt for
many years.

During the 2004 Arab Strategy Forum, I remember
telling Arab leaders loud and clear that if they did not carry
out radical reforms with tangible benefits for citizens,
their people would forsake them and history would judge
them harshly. I advised them to bring about change or
accept that they themselves would be changed.

I was not foreseeing the unseen, for God alone may
know what the future has in store. I was simply drawing

on lessons from our history, which gave a clear indication of what was bound to happen. For every action there is a reaction, and every incident has repercussions.

I remember visiting some leaders and telling them frankly what was likely to happen. Some of them became angry and replied that none of that was mentioned in their briefing reports. So I said to them, "Your problem lies in your briefing reports. This is my honest advice to you and it is not driven by any motives." I only had the Arab peoples' best interests at heart.

I also reasoned with other leaders, saying, "You took over by revolution and now you need to provide a revolution for your citizens. You should give them something. Your people are ultimately seeking a life of dignity, and you should spend all that you have on them and give them all that you can." Their excuse at that time was that they did not have anything to give, knowing full well that they personally were not short of money.

They thought their people would continue to believe them. You can lie to your people for a year or perhaps for two, but surely not for ever. The biggest problem was that they themselves believed their own lies, and forced their press and media to highlight only the positive aspects of the situation. They ended up believing these stories and fell under the illusion that no problems existed. The influence of social media was growing, many truths were being unveiled, and people's patience was wearing thin. The explosion was imminent.

I am in no position to judge the old or new governments of these countries; and I am certainly in no position to judge their people or their revolutions. My only wish is for people to achieve stability, security, peace and progress. In saying so, I am also voicing the hopes, wishes and good will that my country holds towards all Arabs.

People want governments that provide excellent healthcare, education, housing, justice and safety. They want real economic development. This is our singular focus when we strive to provide leadership in government services. Until all governments commit their energy to such principles, unrest and crises will continue to shake our world.

11

Fighting terror

Every day we take a step towards delivering economic development, creating jobs, and raising standards of living, we undermine the ideologies of fear and hate that feed on hopelessness.

People are asking about this "new wave of terror in the Middle East". I'm surprised: we're no strangers to terrorism or struggle or conflict in our region. I dearly wish I could claim otherwise. The problems have always been there, the solutions always just as clear as they are today.

If we are to prevent fanatics and terrorists from leading our agenda, we must acknowledge that we cannot extinguish the fires of fanaticism by force alone. The world must unite behind a holistic drive to discredit the ideology that gives the extremists their power, and to restore hope and dignity to those whom they would recruit.

As the battles and wars that have raged in Iraq, Syria

and Afghanistan (and, in history, elsewhere in our region) show, military containment is only a partial solution. Lasting peace requires three bigger ingredients: winning the intellectual battle; upgrading weak governance; and grassroots human development.

Such a solution must begin with concerted international political will. Not a single politician in North America, Europe, Africa or Asia can afford to ignore events in the Middle East. A globalised threat requires a globalised response. Everyone will feel the heat, because such flames know no borders.

Groups such as Al Qaeda and IS are barbaric and brutal organisations. They represent neither Islam nor humanity's most basic values. Nonetheless, they emerge, spread, and resist those who oppose them with ferocity. What we are fighting when we face these types of group is not just terrorist organisations, but the embodiment of a malicious ideology that must be defeated intellectually.

I consider this ideology to be the greatest danger that the world will face in the next decade. Its seeds are growing in Europe, the United States, Asia, and elsewhere. With its twisted religious overtones, this pre-packaged franchise of hate is available for any terrorist group to adopt. It carries the power to mobilise thousands of desperate, vindictive or angry young people and use them to strike at the foundations of civilisation.

It is the same ideology fuelling groups such as Al Qaeda and IS and their affiliates in Nigeria, Pakistan,

Afghanistan, Somalia, Yemen, North Africa and the Arabian Peninsula. What most worries me is that a decade ago, such an ideology was all that Al Qaeda needed to destabilise the world, even from a primitive base in the caves of Afghanistan. Today, adherents of terror groups in destabilised areas of the Middle East have access to technology, finance, potentially huge land bases, and an international jihadist network. Far from being defeated, their ideologies of rage and hate have become stricter, more pernicious, and more widespread.

The destruction of terrorist groups is not enough to bring lasting peace. We must also strike at the root to deprive their dangerous ideology of the power to rise again among people left vulnerable by an environment of hopelessness and desperation. And, on this note, let us be positive.

The solution has three components. The first is to counter malignant ideas with enlightened thinking, open minds, and an attitude of tolerance and acceptance. This approach arises from our Islamic religion, which calls for peace, honours life, values dignity, promotes human development, and directs us to do good to others.

Only one thing can stop a suicidal youth who is ready to die for terror: a stronger ideology that guides him onto the right path and convinces him that God created us to improve our world, not to destroy it. Credit is due to our neighbours in Saudi Arabia in this field for their successes in de-radicalising many young people through counselling centres and programmes. In this battle of minds, it is thinkers and scientists of spiritual and intellectual stature among Muslims who are best placed to lead the charge.

The second component is support for governments' efforts to create stable institutions that can deliver real services to their people. It should be clear to everyone that the rapid growth of the terror groups of northern Iraq and Syria was fuelled by the Syrian and Iraqi governments' failings: the former made war on its own people, and the latter promoted sectarian division. When governments fail to address instability, legitimate grievances and persistent serious challenges, they create an ideal environment for hateful ideologies to incubate – and for terrorist organisations to fill the vacuum of legitimacy.

The final component is to address urgently the black holes in human development that afflict many areas of the Middle East. This is not only an Arab responsibility, but also an international responsibility, because providing grassroots opportunity and a better quality of life for the people of this region is guaranteed to ameliorate our shared problems of instability and conflict. We have a critical need for long-term projects and initiatives to eliminate poverty, improve education and health, build infrastructure, and create economic opportunities. Sustainable development is the most sustainable answer to terrorism.

Our region is home to more than 200 million young people. We have the opportunity to inspire them with hope and to direct their energies towards improving their lives and the lives of those around them. If we fail, we will abandon them to emptiness, unemployment and the malicious ideologies of terrorism.

Every day we take a step towards delivering economic development, creating jobs, and raising standards of living, we undermine the ideologies of fear and hate that feed on hopelessness. We starve terrorist organisations of their reason to exist.

I am optimistic, because I know that the people of the Middle East possess a power of hope and a desire for stability and prosperity that are stronger and more enduring than opportunistic and destructive ideas. There is no power stronger than that of hope for a better life.

12

Nobody benefits from instability

When our region is torn apart by conflict
and division, nobody wins.
We need to focus on peace, not profit.

The UAE has for many years been known as a pillar of stability in the Middle East. Our status as a safe destination for investment is linked to our role as a regional business hub and economic gateway. Recently, questions have been asked about the extent to which we benefit from funds flowing in from the countries affected by the Arab Spring and the recent unrest in the Middle East.

I am bothered by comments in the Arab media about the UAE "deriving benefit from unrest" in other countries. And what bothers me most is the fact that there is no evidence to back up such claims. The UAE is even being described as living off the tensions in other countries – countries that are dear to us and whose stability is our only wish.

First, I would like to say loud and clear that the UAE

does not work this way. We rank among the top countries when it comes to helping other nations to achieve stability, prosperity and development. We also rank among the world's top countries in terms of foreign aid as a percentage of national income.

Second, the UAE economy is built on stable foundations. We are developing a model for achieving sustainable development, rather than temporary development that lives off regional tensions. Our country embraces people from 200 nations, all working, investing and giving the best they have to offer. Every year we welcome more than 10 million tourists from all around the world.

> 66 *Our country embraces people from 200 nations, all working, investing and giving the best they have to offer* 99

Our strategic trade partners do not include any Arab Spring countries. Indeed, none of our top ten partners is an Arab state, apart from the Kingdom of Saudi Arabia. The investments flowing into the UAE come from all over the world and are all published, totalling 30 billion dirhams (around US$8 billion) in 2012. Worldwide investments in the UAE were flowing strongly long before the Arab Spring. They have continued, and will continue, to flow.

Third, real estate and other types of investments made by UAE companies in the Arab Spring countries are far greater than the capital flows that we receive from these same countries.

To those who say that the UAE benefits from regional unrest, I bluntly reply that the UAE would benefit double and triple, were the region stable and free of tensions.

13

Empowering women

Those in the West who consider Arab women repressed will find the opposite to be true in the UAE. Empowered women are the soul of this nation, the driving force of our development.

Some people still wonder about the empowerment of women in our society. Such questions come most often from abroad. My answer is this: we have already moved beyond the phase of empowering women. Indeed, we are empowering society itself through its women; we are empowering our economy by strengthening the role of women; we are advancing government services when women occupy leadership positions; we are launching development projects under the direction of women; we are improving our infrastructure, our health and education services, and even our military by relying heavily on women's roles in these fields.

The strong representation of women in such areas arises naturally from the fact that almost 70 per cent of university graduates are women. This reflects an ongoing process to strengthen the role of women in society. Perhaps this is why we are the top country in the region for gender equality, according to international reports.

Over 65 per cent of UAE government employees are women; over 30 per cent of leadership positions are held by women. I personally could not manage my daily work without women, since 85 per cent of my personal team are Emirati women.

I have said it loud and clear: Beware, men, lest women deprive you of all the leadership positions in the country.

Women are much more central to Emirati life and to the fabric of our society than many people think. Can a person live without a mother or a sister? Can a house overflow with tenderness without a daughter or a wife? Can a society take any step forward without its better half?

Women are also the very heart of our country. We would never have become what we are today, were it not for the contribution of our loyal, confident and ambitious sisters who are in constant pursuit of excellence and progress, armed with strong will and determination.

I have great confidence in Emirati women and deep faith in their capacities. Their achievements speak for themselves and dissipate any possible doubt in this regard. Some time ago, the Cabinet issued an order to include women in the boards of directors of all companies and government bodies in the country. When people asked me about this, I replied that women represent over half the workforce within these institutions, half the customers of these companies and also half the society influenced by the policies of these government bodies, so is it fair that we men take all the decisions in these institutions on their behalf?

We have read in both ancient and modern history about many great figures educated by their mothers and many great women who left their lasting mark on history. We recognise the greatness of women, both at work and at home. A woman who raises great leaders is herself a great leader. Women have great capacity for generosity, giving and compassion.

There is a saying about rain: it produces abundance wherever it falls. It is our job to provide an enabling environment for women to achieve their highest potential. In other words, we must provide the soil that yields the best harvest from this rain. Our job is to provide an environment that unlocks women's potential – one that protects their dignity and femininity, helps them create the necessary balance in their lives, and values their talents and potential. Given this environment, I am confident that women will perform nothing short of miracles.

14

Two long friendships

*Investing in a friendship is an
investment in the future.*

I travelled with my father to America in 1963. You can only
imagine the impact New York had on me as a young man
of fourteen, born and brought up in the small town of Dubai
in a time before electricity or running water. I remember
sitting in the back of a very large car looking up at rows of
unimaginably tall buildings.

My memories of that trip have stayed with me
throughout my life and on that shocking day in 2001 when
New York came under attack, my thoughts went back to
the city that had welcomed a young man from the desert
and introduced him to another world. I am proud that we
could help with the relief effort, donating to the victims'
families but also putting our resources behind the search
for the people behind the atrocity: our solidarity was not

only a gesture, it was important that all humanity stood together against dark forces such as these.

The UAE and America have long been allies and partners, in development and trade as well as in defence and diplomacy. It is clearly an important relationship for both countries that is cemented on a long history of goodwill and mutual understanding and, most importantly, trust.

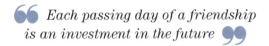

Each passing day of a friendship is an investment in the future

The other long friendship in my life has been with the United Kingdom. When I was a young man, my father was keen I should learn English. He spoke only Arabic and recognised that English was the international language of business and trade.

I first travelled to the United Kingdom in 1966, to study English at the Bell Educational Trust Language School in Cambridge. I had already interacted with British teachers at school, as well as with British children. But nothing prepared me for life abroad. I met with kindness and understanding from people in Britain as I found my feet in a very different culture to my own. I made many friends in the United Kingdom and was to make more on my return to Dubai as our British expatriate community grew with the city. Today there are over 250,000 British expats in Dubai and the UAE is one of the UK's most important trading partners. It is a friendship that goes beyond the lifetime of our young country and one that is deeply important to me.

True friendships stand the test of time. They are cemented by the time we spend together, the support we lend each other, and the trust we build for each other. In a way, each passing day of a friendship is an investment in the future. The more you have shared together, the more you have at stake in your friendship and the stronger it will emerge.

15
Smart Cities

Technology provides unlimited
opportunities to empower people.
Governments must grasp this chance to
become more agile and responsive
to citizens.

Since the dawn of the information age, Dubai has always invested to remain at the forefront of the Middle East's journey towards human development through technological innovation. This journey has always fascinated me. We come to use technologies in ways that surprise even their inventors. Technology has fundamentally changed how we communicate with each other and access information about our world. It seems there is no limit to human ingenuity.

That is what Dubai's Smart City initiative is about: we are harnessing and linking together every available technology that can make people's experience of everyday living in the city simpler, easier, more convenient and efficient. It is about government using technology to help people be happier.

So what is a Smart City? It is about using information intelligently, about making the most of our knowledge and sharing it freely and openly to the betterment of citizens' lives. The possibilities are infinite. We can build a grid of smart water and electricity meters that can all be monitored and managed. We can upgrade schools to gives parents a closer role in their child's education. We can build a transport network that is dynamic and responsive to the flow of people in their daily work and leisure. As a government, we use technology to encourage people to participate actively in shaping policy and services. A Smart City is all of these things together: communication, integration and co-operation.

How could this work? When you fly business or first class with Emirates, the staff greet you by name and know your food and other preferences to offer a highly personalised service because they have access to that data. We are making government work the same way. When you need a government service, the person you are dealing with should have access to all the relevant records without requiring you to stand in line or fill in forms. We are building more dynamic government systems and rolling out new applications that give access to government information, services and resources. This smart approach is core to everything we are building.

Smart government is mobile and agile. We are improving information flows between government departments and also between citizens, businesses and government. That means public–private sector co-operation on a large scale. We aim to provide government services that are equal to or better than our best customer service experiences in the private sector. We are benchmarking government against the best banks, the best airlines, the best hotels.

This challenges traditional thinking. But there is no room for traditional thinking when our goal is to achieve excellence and lead the way to the future.

At the heart of all of this are people. And so our vision for a Smart City has, at its heart, our people.

16

Time management

Time is our greatest asset and our most finite resource. Make every second count.

I have often been asked how I manage my time to get so many things done. I would like to make clear that credit is due to the thousands of people – hard-working teams – who stand behind our accomplishments. I am nothing more than their leader.

As regards time, I say that we all have 24 hours a day. The question is not how we manage our time, but rather how we invest our time. First, there are plenty of tasks that can be performed in less time. For instance, what can be said in a three-hour meeting can be summed up in half an hour, and what can be completed in one month can also be done in one week. Such a skill is indispensable if you wish to achieve more in less time.

On the other hand, time management should be well

balanced, for creating balance in your time entails balance in your life. You should have time for your family, time for your work, time for yourself, time for your hobbies, time for self-development, and so forth.

Time is life and, as such, it cannot be stored or paused. Time is like a flowing river: you cannot step in the same water twice. One of my principles in life is that every minute of our life is worth filling with accomplishments, happiness and good deeds. If you wish to achieve, make the most of every single minute of your life. Never stop working, thinking, innovating and enjoying every single minute, and sure enough, all of this will bear fruit.

> **❝** *Every minute of our life is worth filling with accomplishments, happiness and good deeds* **❞**

Every new day brings new opportunities. Those who do not value every passing minute, every passing hour and every passing day cannot value their life. It saddens me to see young people today spending so much time in coffee shops, watching TV or playing video games, for their time is a great asset to the development and prosperity of our country, society, families and generations.

Some see the year as equivalent to 365 days. Well, I say that a year is equal to the number of days that you have invested in yourself, your family, your society or in your spiritual life. These are the only days that actually count when writing the story of your life. So make the most of them, manage your time, know your priorities, enjoy life, leave your mark and, most importantly, never ever allow anyone to steal your time – for by doing that, they would be stealing your life.

17

Ideas and creativity

*All true creativity brings change.
Embracing change is the first step in
any creative process.*

The fresh thinking that fuels constant progress in government does not come only from the centre and the top, but from all around and from the roots. Employees must be empowered as a source of innovation. Creative ideas are the fruit of interaction between leaders and their teams.

Military leadership has taught me that a commander must listen to his soldiers. Consultation and collaboration are ingrained in our culture. What better example of leadership could there be than that of our Prophet, peace be upon him, who always took heed of his companions' views?

Ideas come from all kinds of people: citizens and residents, children and adults, officials and employees. Everyone contributes ideas, no matter how simple. I have the habit of asking everyone I meet to provide me with fresh ideas that may contribute to our development.

I will digress a little to highlight the importance of creativity. Creativity is the most valuable asset in any public institution. Without it, you can never challenge your past achievements, change your current situation or surpass others.

Progressive governments embrace creativity. It is the lifeblood of our quest to improve services, advance our people and develop our country. A creative government is a living system that grows and develops. In 2012 the UAE government was able to come up with more than 20,000 fresh ideas. Some of our officials talk about creativity and place suggestion boxes in their institutions, thinking that this renders them creative. It doesn't. In order to produce genuine, meaningful, beneficial change, creativity must become an established culture with integrated systems.

Creativity can never thrive in an institutional environment that does not favour learning and the dissemination of knowledge. Nor can it thrive in an institution that resists change or fails to encourage the clear and transparent exchange of ideas and views. I know an institution that was able to increase its returns by 100 million dirhams (around US$27 million) and to cut costs by 240 million dirhams (around US$64 million) thanks to creativity. The key to this achievement was this: the institution began rewarding employees according to their creative contributions.

I was once asked how to become creative. I replied that we should get accustomed to not getting accustomed. Accustoming yourself to a situation gives you comfort, whereas change requires hard work and getting out of your comfort zone. People are not usually fond of change and tend to fight those who call for it, because it requires them to change their habits.

To all creative minds, I say: you will always find someone who will fight your ideas. This will be the first indication that you are on the right track. To all managers, I say: do not fight change – embrace it.

18
Taking risks

To take risks and fail is not a failure.
Real failure is to fear taking any risk.

The UAE is well known worldwide for its remarkable pace of development. When people see ambition and construction on this scale, when they see us launch major projects and plans even amid global economic challenges and regional instability, they often ask: "Don't you find that risky?"

My reply is that no project was ever achieved without risk. Every kind of work entails a certain degree of risk. So, do we stop our life and work? Even banks entrusted with people's money run risks. So, do we stop banks from operating? Going to work by car we are taking risks. Travelling by plane we are also taking risks. So, do we stop going to work or travelling?

Certainly not. Life is full of risks. How can we achieve

our objectives, boost our economy and ensure people's happiness if we do not launch new projects and take some calculated risks?

Challenges are omnipresent and so are risks. Whoever perseveres towards his goals will surely achieve them. Whoever comes up with excuses to stop growing will never be short of excuses.

With each new project or idea that we launch, I face the same questions about risk. I always repeat that the greatest risk of all is not to take any risk. It is true that we never launch a project that is not thoroughly examined and researched; however, we refuse to instil fear into our minds and into our teams.

We refuse to magnify the risks surrounding us. We refuse to be hindered from working, building and growing, even with tensions, unrest and wars going on around us. Our region has witnessed three significant wars in the past three decades. If we had waited for stability to be restored before launching our large projects, where would we stand today?

The best response to regional tensions and also to international challenges in the global economy is to work faster and to complete bigger projects than ever. Development favours stability. When economies are less stable, they can be boosted and anchored by large projects.

Our region and its peoples are in dire need of a successful model in the Arab world – one that gives them hope and proves that focusing on growth is far better than focusing on wars; that launching projects is far more useful than launching rockets; and that building the future is only possible by consensus, reconciliation and team spirit.

Every nation can harness the energy of its citizens, either towards constructive work to generate optimism and hope, or towards tensions, unrest and war.

Arabs are smart people and I am optimistic for the region's future, despite all the tensions it is currently witnessing.

> 66 *You cannot discover new oceans*
> *if you lack the courage to lose sight*
> *of the shore* 99

I would like to move on to another dimension of risk-taking, that is, taking risks at a personal level.

A person who does not take risks in life will avoid difficulties, problems and loss; but he will never mature or learn new things. He will never change. He will never even dare to love. In short, he will never live his life to the full. There is a saying that you cannot discover new oceans if you lack the courage to lose sight of the shore. Life is full of experiences, people, places and adventures; by avoiding risks, you will lose out on all of this.

Quite often we see two people coming from the same background, having received the same education and enjoying the same level of intelligence – but one of them is far more successful than the other. Why is that? It is because one person dared to cement his ideas into reality, to experiment with his innovative side and to transform his life, while the other did not have such courage.

To take risks and fail is not a failure. Real failure is to fear taking any risk.

19
The Burj Khalifa

*Take pride in the scale of your
ambitions. Have faith in your ability to
execute them.*

Why did we want to build the tallest tower in the world?
Why aspire to such a difficult feat of engineering and
construction? The Burj Khalifa is indeed more than just a
construction project. It is a story to which thousands of
people have contributed and a powerful symbol of progress
in our nation.

The drawings that I first received were for an 80-storey
tower surrounded by a few smaller buildings, as well as
gardens and green spaces. I concluded the first meeting
with the project team without commenting on the plans,
so the project team knew they would have to do better.
They returned a month later with a new plan; still it was
not the best.

I told them: "I want the tallest building that man has

ever made, on this spot. We want it to be the biggest and the best, with the best gardens and fountains, and with hotels and markets that are also the biggest and the best. We want to build the greatest neighbourhood ever known to man."

Today, Downtown Burj Khalifa is a city at the heart of a city, circled by an avenue that is considered among the most elegant in the world. It offers the biggest mall and the tallest water fountain in the world. It contains grand hotels, luxury restaurants and residential towers home to thousands of people. Downtown Burj Khalifa has become a key landmark for all visitors to Dubai and the UAE. The tower turned out to be grand and magnificent, so we chose to name it after a great figure, hence the name "Burj Khalifa", in honour of our President, Sheikh Khalifa.

Foreign officials and the media sometimes ask us why we chose to make it the tallest building. They wonder whether Dubai really benefited from building a tower that cost over US$1.5 billion and as part of an overall project costing US$20 billion. In answer to their questions, I would like to clarify the following three points:

First, building the tallest tower on earth is a national accomplishment, a historic milestone and a key economic turning point. It is a symbol of pride, not only to the Emirati people, but to all Arabs. Four thousand years ago, the tallest buildings known to man were found in our region: Egypt's pyramids were a source of pride and a symbol of the advancement of civilisation. They remained so for millennia until surpassed in height by Lincoln Cathedral in the UK, whose creation marked a new era of civilisation. Today, I hope that Burj Khalifa symbolises the new global changes taking place: a new world where East meets West, where civilisations come together and where human creativity reigns with no heed to geographic, ethnic or religious boundaries.

Thousands of engineers, workers, consultants and others from all over the world worked together to construct this impressive building, and new techniques were used for the first time to reach such heights. This is the United Arab Emirates: a new global hub, where the best minds come together to make the greatest dreams come true. In the years to come, the UAE will become increasingly prominent on the world map, because we are well aware that a new era has dawned upon the world. The future is for those who dare to dream and find the courage to pursue their dreams.

Second, we do not seek to derive great economic benefit directly from this building. Rather, its returns will benefit the economy as a whole. Burj Khalifa has enhanced the image of Dubai in particular and the UAE in general, saving millions of dollars on branding. We now have an integrated city with a landmark known and visited by people from all around the world. In 2012, over 65 million people visited the Dubai Mall, part of Downtown Burj Khalifa. To those who remain unconvinced, we say: the greatest risk of all is not to take risks.

Third, building Burj Khalifa sends a message to our people and to the world. To our people, we say that we can achieve so much; we can be number one worldwide in various fields; we can impress the world. We are no strangers to history and civilisation, and we will pay no attention to those who wish to undermine our confidence in our abilities and our people. To the world, we say that the UAE is a new presence in the global economy, one as firmly established as Burj Khalifa.

20

Challenges

Challenges are to be confronted, not avoided. By overcoming and learning from challenges, we transform them from obstacles to signposts on the path to success.

Life is filled with challenges. The lives of our fathers and grandfathers, and also our own lives, have been this way ever since the inception of the UAE. Growing from a simple country to a global nation did not happen without challenges. Had we ceased to grasp these challenges, our country would have stopped progressing.

In the UAE we have two great role models for stepping up to every challenge that comes our way: our founding fathers, Sheikh Zayed and Sheikh Rashid. Throughout his life, Sheikh Zayed never failed to rise to a challenge. The greater the challenge, the stronger his determination. Thanks to such perseverance, we have been able to conquer each and every challenge that has come our way. We simply never give up.

The greatest challenge that I have ever faced personally has been convincing my teams to believe in my vision and to trust in the change I seek. Words alone are not enough; it is necessary to succeed a few times in order to reassure people that you are on the right track, and to convince them to embrace your vision.

Great men are defined by the challenges they take up. I personally cannot judge an individual's strength and capability, unless I confront him with a challenge, for challenges bring out a person's best and worst sides. They are also the best tool for refining a team. Just as high temperatures remove impurities from gold, challenges purify the capacities and strength of those who take them up.

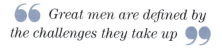

66 *Great men are defined by the challenges they take up* **99**

Since its inception in 1971 the UAE has faced many challenges, both internal and external, but fortunately God gave us strong and wise leaders who stepped up to these challenges, setting an example for their people.

Every challenge is an opportunity for learning, a chance to test our capabilities and knowledge as well as the character of the people around us. Without challenges, victories and achievements would be meaningless.

True experience is measured not by the number of years that we have worked, but by the number of challenges that we have taken up. I sometimes encounter people who hold no academic qualifications, but who enjoy great wisdom and a broad mind, and have more achievements under their belt than many others. The reason is that they have taken up more challenges than others, and their feats bear witness to this.

An easy life does not make men, nor does it build nations. Challenges make men, and it is these men who build nations.

21
Leadership redefined

The keys to leadership lie in the ability
to develop, learn, support and inspire.

Whoever asks the question "Is leadership inherent or acquired?" has already taken his or her first step on the path to leadership. Leadership is a combination of intelligence, resourcefulness, wisdom, a strong personality and aspiration to the greatest of things. Most of these qualities are innate and hereditary, while some can also be acquired. However, even those who are born with such qualities must refine them through education, practice and communication in order to become successful leaders.

Leadership is neither conferred by chance at birth, nor guaranteed by study even at the finest academies. I personally know many graduates from such academies who have worked on themselves and expanded their knowledge to reach high leadership positions, while others stopped at some point because their qualities and skills did not help them to progress any further.

We have seen that an enquiring nature places some people ahead of others on the path to leadership. We also want to change the concept of leadership so that it includes anyone who has the ambition and the will to change himself, and also to benefit his society.

> 66 *Every life you change and every skill you acquire brings you one step closer to becoming a better leader* 99

When we say "leader", people tend to imagine political, military or historical figures who have changed the history of their peoples and countries. They may also imagine successful economic leaders who have transformed companies or given life to new creations and inventions. The hereditary qualities of those people, combined with their environment and their great self-development efforts, have made them exceptional leaders and enabled them to transform their societies and peoples.

But today, the concept of leadership is far wider-reaching. Anyone who can improve the life of those around him is a leader. Similarly, anyone who can serve people and make them happy is a leader. A leader is also a person capable of creating positive change, whether at work or at home, and of innovating and creating even the simplest of things. A leader excels in his craft, art, talent or profession.

All people are born with the seeds of such qualities, which they can nurture and grow, so that bit by bit, they advance on the path to leadership and ultimately evolve into great leaders.

Every single achievement you make, every single life you change and every single skill you acquire brings you one step closer to becoming a better leader. Every day you can improve the leader in you to become a better person and a greater leader.

Were we to limit leadership to exceptional political, economic and scientific figures, we would confine such a vast field to a very limited circle of human beings. Everything can be learnt and every person is capable of self-development. Human development requires entire generations of leaders to lift up their nations and peoples.

A great vision needs not only a great leader, but also a great work team with diverse leadership qualities.

Looking at leadership from this perspective, there is no need to ask whether it is inherent or acquired; rather ask whether one wants to become a leader or not.

22
Endurance

*Know your battlefield. Knowledge is
even more important than capability.*

Endurance horse racing is a popular sport both in the UAE and internationally. It is a testing experience for both horse and rider, with races lasting many hours. In 2012 I was fortunate to win the World Endurance Championships, held in the UK, a great honour for me and a victory that I worked hard to achieve.

This long-distance horse race was organised in the north of the country in unstable weather. Participants came from all around the world: the USA, the UK, Australia, Japan, the Middle East, the Near East and several European countries. There were 150 horsemen from 38 countries in total. The horses were the best and the strongest of their kind. The horsemen were full-time athletes and trainers. All of this added to the tension, especially since I am not a full-time horse rider and practise this sport only as a hobby. Nonetheless, I love horse riding, and I knew my horse and its capabilities well.

I had nominated four horses to pick from and my final choice was one that had never participated in such a large-scale race. I had bought it six years before from a small ranch for a relatively modest sum. I had tried it a month earlier during a small race in Italy, and it was then that I discovered its capabilities. I knew that I could bet on this particular horse because the terrain of the racetrack required a great capacity for ascending and descending mountains.

At the beginning of the race the weather was remarkably unstable, forcing us to cope, in turn, with rain, bitter cold and wind. In an endurance race, you are constantly adapting your plan according to your horse's capabilities, as well as the terrain and length of the race, while trying to keep up with the others. Rushing your horse will tire it, while slowing its pace will keep you behind. If there is a mountain ahead, you should make sure to rest your horse before proceeding; if there is a plain, you can take advantage of the situation to progress, and so on. The challenge lay in balancing all of these variables, but with God's help I was able to come first in this international race, raising the profile of my country and taking home a gold medal.

I would like to draw on my modest experience to give some advice to whoever aspires to attain the title of world champion in any sport, for as people say, it is by teaching others that you broaden your knowledge.

My first piece of advice is to acquire knowledge. You should surpass others in knowledge, for knowledge is the shortest path to victory, even in sports. Know your capacity. Know the capacity of your horse. Know and examine the capacity of your opponents. Know the terrain of the racetrack. Learn its details by heart. Know every part of your horse's anatomy and how it interacts with the racetrack. The more you surpass your opponents in knowledge, the closer you come to beating them into second place.

A race is like a battle. Here I quote the famous Chinese philosopher Sun Tzu, author of the military treatise *The Art of War*: "If you know your enemy and know yourself, you will not be imperilled in a hundred battles; if you know yourself but not your enemy, you win one and lose one; if you know neither your enemy nor yourself, you will be imperilled in every single battle." I would like to add: know your battlefield – for knowledge is more important than capability.

My second piece of advice is training, training and more training. I am not a full-time athlete, but I trained well for this race. I trained my body along the track. I trained my horse to increase its stamina. I trained myself on setting different strategies to reach the finish line. Training opens your eyes to your weaknesses, boosts your self-confidence and brings you a step closer to victory.

My third piece of advice is to trust in God and in yourself, and to be optimistic. These psychological elements are perhaps the most important of all, for they distinguish you from your opponents. Trust in yourself without feeling arrogant or underestimating your opponent. Be optimistic, but do not neglect the smallest details that will ensure your victory. And most importantly, trust in God, for it is God who grants success.

God, of course, knows best about all things. However, I sincerely hope that these few words of advice that I have drawn from my modest experience in sports will be of use to my fellow athletes.

23

Happiness

Good governance is about nothing more or less than creating happiness. It really is that simple.

The job of government is to achieve happiness for people. Indeed, our daily work is all about achieving happiness for people.

When governments evolve and develop services to make people's lives easier, they contribute to their comfort and happiness. When governments create opportunities for people, this makes them happy. When governments offer the best education, they equip young people to build their future and so to achieve happiness for themselves. When governments provide excellent healthcare, patients cannot be happier. When governments develop infrastructure, they reduce the amount of time wasted travelling, which undoubtedly contributes to people's happiness and comfort. When justice is served, the whole society is satisfied and reassured.

There is nothing more beautiful than to create joy in people's hearts. This is our aim in developing services and discovering the best government practices out there. We want to make people happy and we ask God to help us in our quest.

When any official puts his mind to this purpose, his days, his decisions, his projects and even his interactions with people will change completely. Even his self-satisfaction will improve a great deal when he knows that he is contributing to the happiness of thousands of people.

This is what we have learnt from our founding fathers, whose only concern was to lead their people from a life of hardship to a new life of comfort and well-being.

Can you imagine that the gross income of the UAE has increased by over 190 times within just 40 years? Also, that there were only 74 public and private schools in the UAE in 1971? Today, we have more than 1,200 schools. In 1971 the UAE had not more than seven hospitals; today there are 90 hospitals and over 2,000 primary healthcare centres in the public and private sectors. In 1971 the country had no more than 40 graduates and no universities, but thousands of jobs that needed graduates; today, we have 73 colleges and universities with tens of thousands of students. All of this, and much more.

It is clear to me that the driving force behind our founding fathers' tireless efforts was nothing other than their quest to please people and to ensure their comfort. In this way, our leaders succeeded in building a nation, while elsewhere, established countries were destroyed by leaders driven by different priorities. Our leaders have always aimed to please the people and contribute towards their well-being and they have succeeded in doing so. That is why the people love them and show them gratitude.

We could think of happiness as the foundation for many of our ideas and policies. Indeed, some international institutions have even adopted citizen happiness and satisfaction as scientific indicators of development.

We see the government as an active part of society, never as something that is separate or isolated. The government works for the people, achieves its objectives through the people and measures its success through their satisfaction. The government is an authority, but it is an authority at the service of the people and not an authority over them. Its mission is to please them and to build a promising future for their children.

24
Dubai World Expo 2020

*Dubai World Expo 2020 will bring
25 million people from every nation
together under the theme "Connecting
Minds, Creating the Future".*

It is perhaps dangerous to dwell too much in the past – it is the future that holds our attention and potential, not the past. And yet nature places us astride both, the past defining who we are today and the future who we can be if we can harness our potential and qualities.

Dubai World Expo 2020 is rooted firmly in a rich and important tradition and yet it is all about what we can all become.

More than 1,200 years ago, while Europe was in its Dark Ages, the Muslim world was ruled by a dynasty of Islamic leaders who embraced free thought and creativity from all corners of the globe. Never before had history witnessed such cultural openness and symbiosis as during the reign of the Abbasid Caliphs. They built the world's first university, named it Bayt Al Hikma ("House of Wisdom"), and filled its library with the finest cultural, scientific and literary creations known to mankind.

As early as the ninth century, under the Caliph Al Mamoun, Baghdad had become the world's capital of science and culture. The city was renowned for embracing all races and religions. It became a magnet for intellectuals, free thinkers and innovators from East and West. Its people developed a passion for gathering together all of the fruits of mankind's quest for happiness. This celebration of human creativity flourished for more than five centuries and set the stage for the European Renaissance.

Looking at the Middle East and its challenges today, it is tempting to think back to that golden age of Islamic culture with wistful nostalgia for a faraway time. But Al Mamoun's vision is more than ancient history. It is also a solution for the present and the future – a model that we are actively rebuilding, right now.

My own country – the United Arab Emirates – stands where it stands today because since our inception we have given the utmost priority to the human mind. Our land has always been a safe harbour for great thinkers. We have welcomed innovative minds and given them the freedom to create. By working together, thousands of experts and specialists from the UAE and around the world have constructed in Dubai some of the world's most iconic buildings and fastest-growing businesses. In our capital Abu Dhabi, they built the world's largest carbon-free city, complete with advanced research facilities for renewable energy. Great artistic and cultural minds are collaborating to build a vast cultural and artistic city complete with the greatest international museums.

Dubai was founded on trade, not oil. Today, the city is home to the world's busiest and largest airports. We sit at the centre of a global network supported by one of the world's leading airlines, Emirates, and by effective international communications networks. Millions of tonnes of freight come through Dubai's ports and tens of millions of people pass through the city every year.

We travel the seas and skies of the world to drive our trade and to bring ideas, inspiration and innovation to our communities. We are a home to people of over 200 nationalities, a rich resource of culture, creativity and innovation. From this we will foster a spirit of global co-operation and forge links that will endure for millions.

Dubai World Expo 2020 will bring together expert thinkers to share inventive ways to deal with pressing issues such as energy and water supply. Great minds will also come together to share smart solutions for transportation, sustainability and global economic stability.

When we proposed to host the world's biggest cultural event, we promised to astonish the world. Today we pledge to breathe life into our slogan: we will bring minds together for a better future.

We proposed to host this international event in 2020 to deliver three important messages.

Our first message is to tell the world that the Middle East is not a region of conflict, war and tension. Its history and geography prove that this is a region where cultures and civilisations can meet and innovation flourish. Initiatives such as Expo 2020 are an opportunity to restore this role by playing host to the world, communicating positively and openly with its diverse cultures, accepting and embracing ideas and interacting with all people. We are at the heart of the world. Two-thirds of the world's population live less than eight hours away. We are destined to be a meeting point for mankind and a melting pot for cultures and civilisations that will provide humanity with amazing innovations and creations.

Our second message is to the people of our region who are tired of conflict and tension. We tell them that we have a culture, a religion and a language in common: if communication among different cultures can bring about a better future, imagine what it could do for us with all our commonalities. We have been trying for more than six decades to communicate and interact positively within our region.

We have always wanted to establish connections, real connections, to build a better future for the people of our region and its youth in particular. It is time for our region to reclaim its role in history and civilisation. Our history and our culture have destined us for greatness, and our future should showcase this destiny.

We are thankful to the countries that announced their support to us; and to the people of the world our message is that of love and peace. Our slogan will always be that connecting minds creates a better future.

It is a slogan of which Caliph Al Mamoun would have been proud.

25

Opportunities in the Islamic economy

The creativity, beauty and peace of Islam underpin a truly global economic opportunity based on principles of fairness, justice and equality.

The idea of an Islamic economy is based around the principles of social responsibility and fairness that are central to our faith. These principles have influence across all areas of life, and so our approach to the Islamic economy is not only about Sharia-compliant finance and halal food. It also builds on Islamic ideas in areas such as tourism, entertainment, art and design.

The Islamic economy is worth over $6 trillion – a great opportunity, by any standard. But it is also attractive for other reasons. The idea of trading in commodities, ideas and products that are distinctive in quality because they derive from the principles of Islam is one that I find highly appealing.

In January 2013 I outlined a strategy to establish Dubai as the global capital of the Islamic economy, comprising 46 strategic initiatives grouped under seven pillars: finance; halal food; family-friendly tourism; the digital economy; fashion, art and design; economic education; and standards and certification.

Together these pillars provide guidelines for Islamic governance and for a range of innovations, services and offerings that meet the needs of not only Muslims, but those who find aspects of the Islamic lifestyle appealing to them.

You do not have to be a Muslim to appreciate fine calligraphy or a beautifully prepared halal meal. And you do not have to be a Muslim to invest in a *sukuk* – an Islamic finance vehicle – in fact, many Western banks are launching Islamic finance products and that market is sustaining rapid growth.

> 66 *You do not have to be a Muslim to appreciate fine calligraphy or a beautifully prepared halal meal* 99

So the market opportunity goes even further, to the wider world. Dubai is in the ideal position to grow this opportunity as we can address not only Western markets, but the markets of Asia too – a number of which, such as

Malaysia, have large and important Muslim populations.

Not only that, it gives us an opportunity – as Muslims – to show the creativity, beauty and peace of Islam to our fellow men. An ambitious goal, perhaps, but Dubai was built on ambitious goals and I am particularly proud to have set this one for my team in government.

26

Performance

We must not become set in our ways at work. We must stay creative and take risks to drive positive change.

Performance monitoring is one of the most important pillars of successful government. We empower government officials, give them authority and entrust them with budgets. At the same time, we monitor and hold them accountable for their performance. So what happens when an official makes a mistake or falls short? How many chances should he be given? I will examine this question both in terms of the systems that we use to manage and adjust performance across government; and in terms of my personal philosophy for tolerance of mistakes at an individual level.

The first level of monitoring consists of measuring performance according to a strategic plan. We use a comprehensive electronic system that encompasses thousands of performance indicators for measuring the achievements of ministries against their plans. That way, I myself can follow up on the performance of these ministries directly. Every minister can check his ministry's own indicators as well. We send reports to the different ministries on any shortcomings so that they can fix them as they occur.

The second level consists of field follow-up, which means monitoring the level of customer service. We have mystery shoppers and also customers who pay thousands of visits to ministries each year. They prepare reports on customer service that are forwarded to the concerned minister for review and are used to fix any shortcomings.

We too receive copies of these reports, but I do not base my decisions solely on them; hence the third level of monitoring, whereby I personally pay visits to government institutions. I follow up on their projects, check the successful models implemented at some government entities, and meet and listen to second-line and third-line managers. I do not believe in monitoring performance only from the office. Field monitoring gives a better idea of the levels of services and the implementation of policies, and therefore forms an important basis for practical decisions.

Beyond that, we are held to account by layers of independent external checks and audits. Because in the end, we all rally around one national vision – that of ensuring happiness and a decent life for our people.

To err is human and we all fall short in our work

sometimes; but the most important thing is not to be negligent or make errors on purpose. This is the concept that guides our thinking when considering, for instance, how many chances to give an official before dismissing him.

It is by making mistakes that a person learns. If a person falls down, he does not get up where he has fallen, but rather a few steps ahead. Similarly, a person who errs will gain knowledge and experience as a result of his error. This does not mean that we go easy on mistakes, but that we allow some flexibility with loyal and hard-working officers for, I repeat: to err is human.

I might go easy on people who make mistakes, but never on people who make no effort. I do not like our officials to have an exaggerated fear of mistakes. That kind of fear stands in the way of creativity, innovation and change. A few mistakes made by a person working productively cost far less than a person paralysed by laziness or fear.

27

No time to waste

*If you achieve today what you could
have left to tomorrow, you're free
tomorrow to achieve even more.
Why waste the time?*

When people remark on my constant rush to execute projects, I respond that the future starts today, not tomorrow. When people ask, "Why do you want everything now?" I answer, "Why not?" There is no point in waiting. If we wait until tomorrow we will forever procrastinate. So whenever we feel that a project will serve our people, develop our economy and advance our country, we undertake it without delay.

The UAE has transformed itself from an arid desert into a well-developed nation on the global stage in just four short decades. We have never had the luxury of time. We have never accustomed ourselves to waiting. We rush to execute development projects because we believe that a state with economic power also reaps the benefits of political power.

None of our country's achievements would have been possible without the efforts of work teams from every emirate, from Abu Dhabi to Fujairah; or without the participation of every one of our people, from the President to the lowest-ranking employee.

The future does not wait for hesitant people. The more we achieve, the more we realise how much more we can achieve.

Here I would like to recount a personal anecdote. I have got used to inviting the media to dinner each year after evening prayers during the holy month of Ramadan. At these times, we get the chance to discuss different social issues and developments. A few years ago during one of those dinners, a journalist came up to me and asked the following question: "How much of your vision have you achieved so far?" She wanted to know a percentage figure. I tried to dodge the question, but in vain. So after a moment of thought I told her that our ambitions were great, as were the expectations of our people, and that we had accomplished around 10 per cent of our vision.

A couple of years later, at the same time of year and in the same place, the same journalist came up to me and asked the same question. We had recently completed Burj Khalifa, launched Dubai Metro and inaugurated Meydan City, in addition to a host of other impressive projects.

After pondering her question – she once again asked for a percentage – I answered that we had accomplished around seven per cent of our vision. Surprised, she exclaimed, "But your answer was 10 per cent a couple of years ago!" To which I replied, "Of course – for the greater our accomplishments, the wider our vision, the broader our horizons and the clearer our perception."

> 66 *Time is too precious to waste on postponing our people's dreams and expectations* 99

This is a lifelong journey with no finish line. Each time we complete one phase, new possibilities unfold before our eyes. We will continue without halt or rest, for halting is a waste of time. We will pass on the torch for generations to come. We ask God to help us leave our mark on this country and to serve it as best as we can.

Returning to our topic, our objective is to make our people happy and there is no delaying happiness. Time is too precious to waste on postponing our people's dreams and expectations. You just have to multiply the days of delay by the number of people to calculate the years wasted in procrastination. Why waste millions of days of our people's lives in hesitation and waiting? Why defer our people's luxury, happiness and comfort?

They say that rushing is a quality of successful leaders

because their time is precious. Well, I say that rushing is a quality of successful nations that accord due importance to time and due credit to the passing days.

A successful nation forges its own path to success without relying on the situation around it. A successful nation does not wait for the future, but rolls up its sleeves and makes the future. A successful nation does not put off today's work for tomorrow, but starts tomorrow's work today.

28

The brain regain

By attracting the best talent from around the world, we can create a vibrant and diverse society that fuels innovation and prosperity – which in turn attracts still more talent.

In 1968, while studying at the Mons Officer Cadet School in the United Kingdom, I needed to visit a hospital. There I met a doctor who, to my surprise, spoke fluent Arabic. I learned that he was new to the UK, so I asked if he intended to stay long or return home. He replied with an Arabic saying that translates as: "My home is where I can eat."

That doctor's words stayed with me for many years, because they underscored the contradiction between our idealised view of "home" and the harsh realities of life that push talented people to leave.

The doctor was a classic case of the "brain drain" phenomenon that has afflicted developing countries for decades. These countries spend scarce resources educating doctors, engineers and scientists, in the hope that they will become engines of prosperity. Then we watch with dismay as they migrate to the West, taking with them the promise of their talent.

It is, of course, everyone's right to choose a better life, wherever in the world they wish. We understand why they go. Talent is drawn – like a magnet – to opportunity.

For the countries left behind, however, it feels like an endless vicious cycle: they need talent to create opportunity; but without opportunity, talent gravitates to the bright lights of the West. Indeed, the United Nations and the OECD report that migration for work has risen by one third since 2000. One in nine university graduates from Africa now lives and works in the West. Many will not return: skilled workers are six times more likely to stay away.

But now something remarkable is happening: in some countries, the brain drain has reversed its flow. The causes are fascinating, and there is reason to be optimistic that the vicious cycle can be broken, transforming the balance of hope and opportunity between developing and developed economies.

A study by LinkedIn, the world's largest online professional network and recruitment platform, measured the net international movement of talent among its members. Topping the list as a destination for talent is my own country, the United Arab Emirates, with a net talent gain of 1.3 per cent of the workforce in 2013. Other net "talent magnets" include Saudi Arabia, Nigeria, South Africa, India and Brazil.

Most interesting, fewer than one third of net talent importers are developed countries. In fact, the top talent exporters in this study are Spain, the UK, France, the United States, Italy and Ireland. Rich countries that until recently had been tempting away our brightest minds are now sending us their own.

Of course, this is only one study, and many poor countries still suffer from a chronic talent exodus. OECD data show that many countries in Africa and Latin America have migration rates for graduates above 50 per cent.

We do know that brain drain is often a function of safety and security as much as economic opportunity. Part of the tragedy playing out in Middle Eastern countries beset by conflict and instability is that if only their most talented sons and daughters could apply their skills at home, they would become part of the solution: agents of peace through development. This makes it all the more important to examine how some developing countries succeeded in reversing the outward flow.

The basic ingredient is opportunity. Talent flows naturally to countries that create an environment for economic growth; that make life easy for enterprise; that attract and welcome investment; and that nurture a culture of achievement. Skills are attracted to challenge and possibility.

Opportunity on this scale is becoming a scarce commodity in many parts of the West. Not so in the developing world – at least among countries with the appetite and determination to deploy strong governance and continually raise their competitiveness.

Second, quality of life matters greatly. A generation ago, many talented individuals would consider working outside the West a "hardship posting". Today, standards of living in the UAE, for example, are among the highest in the world. We have shown that the business of reversing the brain drain is also the business of creating a better life for citizens and residents. Building happiness is, after all, the primary business of good government everywhere.

Ours is a story of great hope for the Middle East in particular, where generations of conflict and despair have driven high levels of outward migration. I have always argued that, besides good governance, the best solutions to the divisions and strife of the Arab world lie in grass-roots development and economic opportunity. Now, we have shown that it is possible to reverse the forces that had driven away our most talented young people.

Another source of hope: this turnaround can happen remarkably quickly. Research shows that small countries suffer disproportionately from brain drain. But we have shown that even for a small country like the UAE, and even in a region divided by conflict, it is worth building an island of opportunity.

But let me be clear: reversing the brain drain is about

more than plugging a leak. It means flipping a vicious cycle into a virtuous one. By attracting the best talent from around the world, we can create a vibrant and diverse society that fuels innovation and prosperity – which in turn attracts still more talent.

To make this work, we must believe in people. Human beings – their ideas, innovations, dreams and connections – are the capital of the future. In this sense, the "brain regain" is not so much an achievement in itself as it is a leading indicator of development, because where great minds go today, great things will happen tomorrow.

29
Nurturing teams

A great vision can only be achieved by a great team. This is an everyday truth for world-class businesses, and just as true for world-class governments.

Any enterprise faces the same challenge of investing in people, in motivating and developing them, making the most of their talents and helping them to succeed and achieve the best possible results. Nowhere is this as challenging as in government. In driving a process of reform in the UAE's government, we recognise that the most important approach is not centred on punishment or criticism, but on investment and nurturing. Last year alone we invested more than 1.3 million hours in training more than 55,000 federal government employees.

We launched a leadership programme for second-line and third-line leaders, and gave out excellence awards to our employees, since competition among employees brings out the best in them. We replaced the criterion of seniority with the principle of competence in promotion and recruitment. Today it is competence and accomplishment that prevail.

I have three points of advice for public servants.

First, act like a leader, for true leadership is not in one's position, but in one's way of thinking and acting: it is in the nobility of one's objectives and goals. A true leader serves the people, acts in their interests and works for their happiness. A true leader does not need to be supervised in order to devote himself to his work, to achieve and to innovate. He should have an inner impetus that makes him aim for no less than first place.

A true leader does not derive power from his position, but from his ethics, from people's love for him, and from his knowledge, education and excellence in his field of work. To all government employees, I say this: you are all leaders, and therefore you should exceed all expectations.

Second, if you look at civil service as a mere job, you will be a mere employee. You are a leader, not an employee, and this role is more than a job, it is also an opportunity. It is an opportunity to show your talents and capabilities, an opportunity to add new value to your society. It is an opportunity to inspire and influence all those around you. Even more, it is an opportunity to contribute to the making of your country's history. So do not carry out your work as an employee, but as a leader who loves his country, as a craftsman who is passionate about his craft, and as an artist who excels in his art. We expect no less from you.

Third, develop your capabilities continuously, expand your knowledge and broaden your horizon, and never give up on your work. Perseverance is much more important than intelligence. Any improvement on your work, no matter how minimal, could produce remarkable outcomes. So never stop developing yourself and never look back. Always aim at first place and at serving your country and society.

> 66 *A true leader serves the people, acts in their interests and works for their happiness* 99

We constantly encourage government officials to achieve more. We continuously offer opportunities in training, development and the exchange of knowledge and expertise, both locally and abroad. We give officials one chance after another to develop themselves – but not indefinitely. There comes a time when we have to thank an official for his work and give someone else a chance to pump new blood into our institutions. Such is life, and such is the business of government.

Only achievers who are able to keep up with change

and are ready to take on challenges and bring out the best in their teams will stay. Only innovative and creative officials with wide horizons, great determination, positive energy and optimism will stay. Every official knows himself or herself, and ultimately it is the people who bear witness to our achievements. Therefore, I should not be the one to judge. Let them be accountable to themselves, and to the people, for their actions.

May God grant us all success in the service of our country and people, and in our mission to raise the profile of the UAE.

30

The government of the future

We have seen what happens to governments that resist change and do not listen to their people. It is by working in the service of our people that we earn their trust.

What will government look like in the future? Before delving into the subject, I would like to point out that when we talk about the government of the future, we focus on the delivery of services and not on political structures. Different countries have diverse forms of government. However, they all should work towards one goal: serving citizens.

How can a government be closer to its people, faster, better and more responsive in providing its services? This is my first and foremost concern, and this is the main focus of our development efforts in the UAE.

Some time ago we received a delegation from the Japanese government. They wished to learn from our experience in providing a particular government service: land and property registration. In some countries this is a complex process that can take months or even years. When I told one of my colleagues about the visit, he was impressed by our achievement in creating a system so efficient that advanced nations such as Japan would like to emulate it. "I think you have reached the finish line, Your Highness," he said. "Your teams deserve to celebrate and rest after such a dazzling success."

I disagreed. My recipe for success is continually to raise the bar whenever we reach our goals. It is right to feel proud of such achievements, but we may never feel satisfied. We must always aim higher in order to sustain our ambition and achieve excellence. So I replied: "Our definition of success has changed. We must look ahead now to the next generation of governments."

So, what will the government of the future look like?

Service-oriented

The government of the future is open for service 24/7, all year round. The private sector remains open for business so why not the public sector? We want our government to be just like an airline – available around the clock.

Businesslike

The government of the future competes with and surpasses the private sector in service quality. We want our government to welcome customers more professionally than hotels; we want our government to manage processes better than banks.

Connected

The government of the future is connected. Citizens should be able to complete any government transaction at any government service centre. Integrated service centres will spare citizens long trips from one entity to another.

Available

The government of the future is available everywhere. We want to shift government services onto smartphones so that customers can file and follow up on transactions using mobile devices, at their convenience.

Innovative

The government of the future is innovative and constantly able to generate ideas. In 2012 the UAE government was able to generate over 20,000 fresh ideas to simplify and improve its services. Our goal is to create an environment that encourages people to generate innovative ideas,

implement them and constantly measure their effective-
ness. Innovation is the capital of the future.

Smart

The government of the future is a smart government
with integrated and efficient technical systems. A smart
government is so much faster in completing various kinds
of transactions.

We have already begun working on many of these ideas
and, in the years to come, people will start to feel the
benefits in their everyday lives. At that point, we will
start to consider a new definition for success in providing
government services.

31

Aid to the world

Helping those less fortunate than us is a blessed opportunity to show thanks for the gifts of life that we ourselves enjoy.

The UAE has a proud record of providing assistance to people in other countries who find themselves afflicted, destitute or otherwise less fortunate than us. Since its inception in 1971, the UAE has provided an estimated 160 billion dirhams (around US$43 billion) in foreign aid. Annual foreign aid is equivalent to around one per cent of our gross national income. These figures place us at the forefront of foreign aid contributions worldwide.

It is against our customs and morals to brag about helping others, but still I feel the need to explain our approach to foreign aid and its catalysts, both for the record and also to set an example to other countries and to future generations.

It all started with the Father of our Nation. Sheikh

Zayed is at the root of our generous nature and his name has become synonymous with true giving.

Sheikh Zayed does not need our testimony, for the cities of Palestine, the hills of Pakistan, the plains of Morocco and Egypt, the dams of Yemen, the villages of Bangladesh and many, many other places bear witness to his generosity. Even the Holy Land of Jerusalem and its surroundings bear witness to his good deeds.

It is Sheikh Zayed, God bless his soul, who instilled benevolence in our hearts, taught us the principles of giving, and accustomed us to doing good deeds.

Generous by nature and compassionate at heart, such is our President, Sheikh Khalifa. It is no wonder that in one year, more than half of UAE foreign aid came from a single source, the Abu Dhabi Fund for Development, under the directives of Sheikh Khalifa. That fund alone contributed 4.9 billion dirhams (around US$1.3 billion) to UAE foreign aid in just one year, not to mention the Khalifa Foundation and other charities working directly under Sheikh Khalifa.

The Emirati people do not live in luxury and isolation from the world around them. On the contrary, we are a vibrant people, we empathise with the suffering of others. We contribute positively to alleviating their pain, helping those in need, and fighting poverty, hunger and sickness on earth.

We give without hesitation. When the global financial crisis struck the world in 2008 and many countries curbed their charitable and humanitarian donations, the UAE went against the tide and actually increased its foreign aid.

We believe that giving knows no limits. As such, 95 per cent of our aid is not recovered to avoid burdening the economies of less fortunate countries.

We also give unconditionally. Our purpose is strictly humanitarian, untouched by political agendas, geographical boundaries or ethnic, racial or religious discrimination.

We strive to be an international humanitarian capital and a beacon of hope for all those in need. The UAE is not just a financial and economic nucleus, neither is it just a tourism hub: we are also a nerve centre of global humanitarian work.

We will always be there to lend a helping hand to our brothers and friends, and to the destitute and the needy, wherever they might be.

This is our message to the world.

32

Governing a people

The UAE's system of governance is not only effective – it is highly accountable.

I am sometimes asked about democracy and our system of governance in the United Arab Emirates, which is perhaps different to what some Western observers may expect. But it has evolved as a result of the way our young nation has evolved and grown.

Dialogue is crucial to our society, not only as a way of passing down knowledge and cultural identity to younger generations, but also as a way of exploring our goals together and resolving our differences. Listening, dialogue, participation and accountability are deeply rooted principles of Emirati society. They are cultural institutions.

Democracy is one of many political systems intended to involve the people in governance that serves their well-being. The UAE has evolved a different political system serving that same principle. It was born in early times when this region was home to nomadic tribes and small trading communities. A leader was found from within the community, someone who everybody agreed they could trust to serve the needs of the community.

We have a great institution, the majlis, a traditional open forum where leaders listen to the grievances, problems, ideas and blessings of their people. This guarantee of access to the ruler enables people to seek fairness, justice and restitution when they are confronted by challenges in life. People come to the majlis with suggestions, opinions and opportunities. In the modern world, people call this "crowdsourcing". It has always been a key element in our community and society.

> 66 *A strong ruler acting for the benefit of a unified people can achieve great things with great speed* 99

My father's public majlis was held on a seat outside his house in the old Shindaga area of Dubai. He was able to direct progress and take the counsel of those most closely involved with the development of Dubai. He governed while keeping the needs of the people as a whole in mind, adjudicating disputes and establishing principles for the community to follow. It is important to remember this idea of service to the community.

Governance through a majlis alone is no longer feasible: our modern world is too complex; the scale of our nation today is too great. We have many institutions to help serve our people in all aspects of their daily lives, from law courts and regulators through to the Federal National Council, which connects government to the people.

The principles of accountability and service are embedded within our system of government. The ruler has the well-being and benefit of his people in mind at all times. It is not a position of privilege, but one of service and responsibility. In such a system, the ruler is no less accountable than a politician in a Western-style democracy.

A strong ruler acting for the benefit of a unified people can achieve great things with great speed. We are not caught up in endless debate – the path forward is clear. And yet we are answerable to God and to our people for our actions and decisions.

33

A child's dream

Horsemanship is a noble calling that brings out the best in a leader.

A small child once asked me how he could become a horseman like me.

I told him that, by asking this question, he had already taken the first step on the right path, for it is said that questions account for half of one's knowledge. Horse riding is not just a sport; it represents high morals, nobility, chivalry and excellence. Horse riding starts from the inside.

I told this child that the first lesson in horse riding is that he should love and obey his parents, excel at school, respect his elders and possess a horseman's qualities of vigour and chivalry, among others. It is only when he acquires such attributes and when his parents, his teachers and the people around him are satisfied with his high morals that the easier part of learning how to ride a horse in clubs and other training facilities can follow.

A child's love for horse riding expresses his high ambitions and great determination. I always encourage our little ones to ride, for I have seen the great influence of this sport on them. Some 1,400 years ago, Omar ibn Al Khattab, one of the four Righteous Caliphs in Islam, observed: "Teach your children swimming, archery and horseback riding." He was an Arab horseman, a wise leader and one of the greatest figures in history. So his advice regarding horse riding did not come out of nowhere; rather it establishes a solid relationship between horse riding and dignity, pride, chivalry and high morals.

Horse riding embodies a strong bond between the horseman and his horse, as well as a synchronisation between the horseman's movements and the horse's progression. It teaches the horseman patience, strength, control and speed – qualities that should grow in our children. Inner morals harmonise with outer qualities, just as self-confidence harmonises with speed of movement and strength. The force of the emotions that bond the horseman to his horse is reflected in the qualities of endurance and patience that develop.

The relationship of Emirati people to horses comes from our authentic Arab roots and this perpetuates the sport of our ancestors. Today, horse riding represents our Arab and Islamic identity, our pride in our heritage and our high morals, which we are instilling in our younger generations. Only goodness comes from horses; as the Prophet, peace be upon him, said: "Goodness is tied to the forelocks of horses until the Day of Resurrection." Horse riding is an everlasting sport. Only good people treat horses with kindness and only great spirits seek and practise horse riding.

34

A sound leader in a sound body

Only those who are fit in body, mind and spirit may truly aspire to lead others.

I was once asked if there is any link between leadership and taking part in sports. My reply was, "Can you imagine a lazy or inactive leader?" A leader should be fit, healthy and athletic. He should be both mentally and physically active. He must have a strong build and a sharp mind. Hence I say, "a sound leader in a sound body".

Personally, sports are an essential part of my daily schedule. If I am not fully energetic and healthy myself, I will not be able to get my team moving. Not only do sports develop your body muscles, they build your mind's muscles as well. I walk no less than three kilometres a day, 10 kilometres once a week, and 20 kilometres once a fortnight.

Besides walking regularly, I practise different hobbies such as horse riding and cycling. My daily workout does not hinder my productivity in any way, since I carry out my work over the phone while exercising.

My advice to all is to practise sports on a regular basis, for the quality of your life is related to the quality of your health, and your level of achievement in life depends on how energetic and active you feel. It is said that health is a treasure; well, I say that if time is life, then health gives meaning to our time and adds spice to life.

It bothers me to hear, watch and read about the many cases of cardiovascular disease, hypertension and diabetes due to lack of exercise. Our modern life of luxury offers all sorts of treats and delights. Our ancestors did not suffer from the diseases which are widespread today, and the main reason was their active life and the nature of their work.

I sometimes encounter groups of women out walking for exercise. I am so overjoyed to see this that I stop for a few moments to encourage them to keep up this good habit, and exchange a few words. I was once speaking about these moments and the importance of workouts and self-discipline in eating. The person I was talking to replied that he personally could not resist food and neither could he commit himself to working out. I replied, "Those who have control over themselves can control the world around them, unlike those who do not have self-control."

Some make their busy schedule an excuse for not

working out; I wonder of what use their money will be to them if their health fails. Others give researching, learning and reading as an excuse; I wonder if their education will be any good to them without good health. Nothing in your life, not even the quality time you spend with your family, could be complete without good health.

And so, I end with the simplest of advice: make time in your life for exercise, for this is the soundest investment that can be made in health, future and happiness.

35

The gift of life

Make time to take in the richness
and beauty of life.

Life is an extraordinary gift some people appear not to appreciate. In every breath and scent, every touch and sight, we are gifted with new experience and the chance to feel the richness of experience. Every sound we hear, from the song of a bird to the harshness of an angry voice, is a miracle.

Sometimes it is hard to remember the joy of this gift. When we are burdened by care or perplexed by circumstance, it is easy to close off our senses to things that would normally bring wonderment and pleasure. We focus instead on the negative, the thing that is confounding us, for whatever reason.

I have often found the key to a challenge lies in meeting it and rising above it, by seeking alternative solutions. And it is harder to do this if you have closed yourself off to all around you. This is the way to negativity and despair. It is important to remember the gift we have, each and every one of us. Be bright-eyed, attentive and open to new ideas and experiences – reach out and enjoy the life you have. The solutions to your problems will come more easily, trust me.

I thank God for the gift of faith, too. I was brought up in a religion, Islam, that shows me a way of life and gives me clear values and guidance in my life. To sit in the peace and solitude of the winter desert and give your thoughts up to God is an experience I treasure above all else. The problems of the world are cast away and one feels truly alive at this time. Life's challenges are always put into perspective: they are insignificant compared with the greatness of the gift of life.

> 66 *Be bright-eyed, attentive and open to new ideas and experiences – reach out and enjoy the life you have* 99

The ability to live in a stable, safe environment that gives us the opportunity to create, grow and nurture our talents is sadly denied to many in the world today. Those of us that enjoy these privileges should not hesitate to make the most of what we have.